S0-BII-578

# Real Estate Uncensored

## Game Changing Insights
## From a Real Estate Insider

**Gayle Barton**

**Copyright © 2017 Real Estate Uncensored: Game Changing Insights from a Real Estate Insider by Gayle Barton**

All rights reserved. Printed in the Unites States of America. No part of this book may be used or reproduced in any manner whatsoever without written permission except in the case of brief quotations embodied in critical articles or reviews.

This book is for educational and entertainment purposes only.

Book and cover design by Prominence Publishing.

For information, contact www.ProminencePublishing.com

Gayle Barton can be reached at www.BartonTeamRealEstate.com

ISBN: 978-0-9958274-1-7

# Contents

# Foreword

In my 37 years in the real estate industry I have seen and heard many things which have shocked me but, time and time again, I have witnessed Gayle's venerable experience allow her to handle each test with total aplomb.

Her unwavering attention to her clients' needs, and understanding of the stress that naturally comes with selling or buying a home, motivates her to doggedly oversee each step of the process in an effort to create a seamless and stress-free transaction for each and every one.

Beyond her personal dedication and recognized marketing prowess, I must admit that I remain most impressed by Gayle's desire to continuously educate herself in an effort to remain on the cutting edge of our industry's ever changing technology. If I were selling my home, I would want Gayle representing me!

- Kaylin Pound, Sr. Vice President/Regional Managing Broker, Berkshire Hathaway HomeServices Georgia Properties

# Introduction

In 1983, Texas had just experienced one of the worst oil busts in history and people were literally walking away from their homes. At that point, mortgage rates ranged from 13 to 18% depending on your credit. Why I thought that was the right time to jump into real estate I'm not sure, but it was certainly the right time to learn an extraordinary life lesson.

While that introduction led to lots of nights eating boxed macaroni and cheese, it taught me how to work hard and push for success even when the going is tough. **Basically, you can't have "million dollar club" success with a minimum-wage work ethic!**

In 1989, when I moved to Georgia I knew nothing of the local real estate market so I chose to take a job in corporate America. The tech industry was beginning to grow by leaps and bounds and my natural aptitude for technology led me straight in that direction. I did obtain my Georgia real estate license in 1990, but decided to use it only to help myself and my friends. Looking back, I realized that it was an excellent decision as it kept me current on changes in the real estate industry.

After many years in the IT field, the birth of my son in 2000 led me to want a more flexible schedule and I wanted to work in an industry I loved. So, in 2002, I headed right back to real estate.

One of the things I found most intriguing about my decision to re-enter the real estate industry was the fact that my technology background now proved to be a major benefit. In college I studied marketing and when I added my technology skills on top of that I found that I could offer my clients a significantly higher level of service than most of my competitors.

In 2002, I started a property management company that allowed me to help my buyers and sellers continue to receive service from me even after their closing. After a year the company had grown so large that my husband chose to quit his corporate job and join me as my real estate partner.

In 2009, we sold the management company and I refocused my energy to supporting homebuyers and sellers reach their real estate related goals. Over the next few years I redoubled my efforts to create a top producing real estate marketing team.

I offer my clients 30+ years of negotiating experience.

For my BUYERS, this specialized knowledge allows me to assist you in locating the perfect home, in the perfect area, for YOUR family.

For my SELLERS, my specialized knowledge allows me to market your home to the buyers most likely to purchase a property in your neighborhood

I am well known for my use of innovative technologies in successfully marketing properties and matching buyers with the properties that most closely fit their needs. But, despite my use of the most up to date high tech "gadgets", I still believe that personal service is at the forefront of my success!

I feel confident that you will find no other agent more willing to put your needs first and provide the level of service you require. My goal is to provide the highest level of service possible without compromising honesty or integrity.

My clients' needs are my number one priority and putting them first is how I distinguish myself from other agents in my area. I pride myself on providing personalized service to each and every client with honesty, integrity and enthusiasm. Through my dedication to service I have earned the respect of our previous clients, developing a rapport which has allowed me to build a business based strongly on referrals. I feel confident that you will find no other real estate team more willing to put your needs first and provide the level of service you require.

# Chapter One

# Choosing an Agent to Sell Your Home

Selling your home is an important business decision so you will want to work with an industry professional. Personal referrals from friends or business colleagues are always an excellent place to start, but you will definitely want to vet them as thoroughly as you would anyone applying for a job.

My biggest motivation for writing this book is the fact that I feel many real estate consumers are being grossly underserved by what I call "hobbyists". You would never go to a part-time doctor or a part-time dentist so I believe it is important that you understand the detrimental affect using a part-time real estate agent can have on the outcome of your real estate transaction.

I would strongly recommend starting with an Internet search for their name plus the term real estate and the name of your town (ex: Gayle Barton real estate Cumming GA). This is an easy way for you to determine the strength of their Internet presence.

> **Hint**: If you can't find them on the Internet, buyers are not likely to find their property listings either.

**Spend time on their website:** Is it attractive and professionally designed to keep a buyer engaged? Does it provide information other than just home listings? Does it feel welcoming?

**Read their reviews:** I believe that one of the best sources for agent reviews is Zillow. Zillow actually verifies the veracity of each review submitted so no one can have friends or family members pump up their numbers with false reviews.

**Check out their social media:** Do they have a professional/business Facebook page, Twitter page, etc... Are they active on LinkedIn? These are all excellent sources of buyer leads and should be utilized as part of a robust internet marketing program.

Once you have narrowed your search down to two or three agents you will want to set up interviews with each one. Allow yourself at least two hours for each interview. You may not need to spend that much time with each candidate, but you do not want to be hurried if you find an agent you would like to spend more time with but the next one is already knocking at the door.

Keep in mind that you will spend a great deal of time working with this person and putting a great deal of trust in them. You want someone who not only demonstrates knowledge and professionalism, but also someone with whom you feel comfortable sharing your personal story.

## The Interview Process

It only makes sense that, once you decide to sell your home, you would thoroughly interview the listing agents you are considering for the job. Below is a list of the questions I recommend you ask all prospective listing agents during the interview process.

### *"Are You A REALTOR®?"*

Many of my clients are surprised to learn that there is a major difference between a "real estate agent" and a "Realtor®". A Realtor® is a member of the *National Association of Realtors* and, usually, a local board of Realtors as well. Both of these entities require that a Realtor® uphold the standards of the association and its strict code of ethics.

> **Hint:** This means that a real estate agent who has not chosen to become a Realtor® is **not bound by any ethical code whatsoever**. While this does not in any way mean that they are a terrible person, it does mean that, as a consumer, you have one less level of protection on your side when choosing to do business with them.

### *"Are You A Full-Time Agent?"*

This may very well be the most important question you will ask during the interview process!

**If the answer is "no",** you should more than likely end your conversation at this time as working with a part-time agent can greatly limit your home's availability. If your agent is not available to take calls from buyer's agents to answer questions, provide information/documents or set showing appointments, this limits the ability of a buyer's agent to show and sell your home. Many will simply move on to an easier sale.

**If the answer is "yes",** be sure to ask what days and hours the agent works. You may be surprised to find that many agents consider themselves to be full-time but limit their working hours or choose to work only Monday through Friday. While this is great for their work/life balance, it makes it very difficult for buyer's agents to contact them in their "off time", again potentially limiting your home's saleability as many buyers look for homes solely after normal office hours or on the weekend.

If an agent tells you that they limit the number of days or hours that they work, the next question should be, "Who handles your business when you are unavailable and exactly how does that work?"

> *Hint:* Your goal here is to determine just how easy it is for an appointment to be made by a buyer's agent or for information to be passed to them. Also, you want to know if the listing agent is available to show your home to a buyer not currently working with a buyer's agent.

### *"What Certifications Do You Hold?"*

Most Realtors® have a string of letters behind their name that mean little to the average consumer. However, when you are interviewing agents to represent you in the sale of your home there are a few that you should be aware of.

**CRS** – A "Certified Residential Specialist" has invested significant time, money and energy to complete additional courses of training and have demonstrated a proven track record for residential sales. Nationally, only 3% of Realtors®

hold this designation and it is the mark of an agent who is dedicated to real estate as a professional.

**e-PRO** - An e-Pro certified agent has completed additional training through the National Association of Realtors® designed to enhance their ability to fully utilize technology in the promotion of their listings online. With over 90% of all buyers starting their home search online, this designation displays an agent's ability to more professionally market your home through the use of technology.

**SRS** - A "Seller Representative Specialist" has completed additional training through the Real Estate Business Institute designed to elevate professional standards and enhance personal performance.

**CLHMS** – The "Certified Luxury Home Marketing Specialist" designation is recognized as the mark of accomplishment in luxury markets around the world. Agents holding this designation consistently perform in the TOP 10% of their markets in regard to sales volume, and have successfully demonstrated their expertise in the luxury home and estate market.

> **Hint:** Holding multiple designations is one indication that an agent considers real estate to be their profession, not their hobby.

### *"How Many of Your 'PERSONAL LISTINGS' Did You Close Last Year?"*

This question is important because many agents are now part of a team. You are concerned with the actual, individual production of the agent sitting in front of you. Your goal is to determine what this person is going to do to help you get your home sold for the most money possible, in the shortest time possible and with the least hassle possible. You are not looking for the number of listings closed by the team, but the percentage of this agent's personal listings which resulted in a closed sale.

### "How Many LISTINGS Did You 'PERSONALLY' Service Last Year?"

While many agents want to tout the fact that that they are the "#1 listing agent" or they "list the most houses in their office", you will want to fully understand the details of that claim. Harkening back to the previous question, if they personally listed 20 properties but only 10 of those properties actually sold, this may mean that their marketing program is weak or that they are simply spread too thin.

> **Hint:** You are looking for an agent with a proven track record of closing a high percentage of their listings and who has both time and energy to dedicate to the sale of your home. Too many listings may mean that they simply will not have enough time available to dedicate themselves to you. Too few listings may mean that they don't yet have the experience needed to fully support your listing.

## *"What Price Do You Want To List My Home For?"*

Okay, they've proven their track record in terms of selling the homes they list. Now you want to verify their ability to properly price your home to place it "in the market" not "on the market". If homes around you are selling for $200,000 you can put your home "on the market" for a million dollars. It is unlikely to sell, but it will be "on the market".

To price your home "in the market" a knowledgeable agent will provide documented sales and market data from multiple sources to help educate you on the current state of market and suggest a list price. While the seller always determines the list price, a smart seller will price their home within the range suggested by the market data analysis reports.

Many sellers want to "test the market" by pricing their home above the market value suggested by the sales data or listing agent. Because the majority of showings occur during the first three weeks of a home hitting the market, this may ultimately result in a lower sales price than would have been realized had the property been priced appropriately from the start. In many cases, by over pricing the property the seller inadvertently places his home in direct competition with larger or more upgraded homes, which only serves to make the competing homes look more appealing by comparison. Additionally, the buyers who would have gladly purchased the home are now lost as they never saw the home because it fell outside their price range search parameters.

> **Hint:** Do not be tempted to hire an agent simply because they are willing to agree to a higher list price. In the industry, this is called "buying the listing". These agents know that you will eventually reach a point where you're forced to

lower the price in order to sell. Unfortunately, when this happens the listing becomes stale and many buyers become leery that the property may have issues which can result in lower offers. Additionally, and in some cases most detrimentally, you will have wasted time and money in terms of mortgage payments made during the wasted months.

## *"Do You Live In This Area - IS THIS YOUR PRIMARY MARKET?"*

As a licensed real estate agent in Georgia I can legally list and sell property anywhere in the state. However, I choose to limit my market area to the county in which I live and a small portion of the contiguous counties surrounding it. While that may seem somewhat limiting, I do this because I believe that an agent should have extensive knowledge of the communities they serve – quality of schools, proximity to healthcare providers, etc. I pride myself on being an "area specialist". I feel that limiting the scope of my service area allows me to better understand the needs and wants of the local buyer demographic and market your home directly to them.

If you are dealing with an agent who does not consistently work in your local market, they may offer limited knowledge in terms of properly pricing your home - either too high or too low - or lack the understanding of how best to market your home to the buyers most likely to purchase a property in your neighborhood.

## *"What Is Your Marketing Plan For My Home?"*

Now we're getting down to the nitty-gritty. **While most sellers think they are hiring a listing agent, what they are really doing is hiring a marketing professional!**

For obvious reasons, most agents are reluctant to share their "secret sauce" without a signed listing agreement in hand, but you will want them to provide you with a detailed, property-specific marketing plan that clearly demonstrates what they will do to make your home stand out from the competition and grab the attention of active buyers, both online and in print.

- Will they provide professional photography or will they be taking the photos themselves? How many photos are included? For large or specialty properties do they utilize videos or drone technology?

- Do they provide a virtual tour? Can they show you an example online?

- Do they provide professionally printed, color brochures and marketing collaterals or do they print brochures in their office? Ask to see an example.

- Do they offer a professionally designed, mobile friendly, website where photos of your home will be displayed online? Do you have multiple sites or only one?

- How do they promote your web listing? Where?

- Where and how do they advertise your property?

### *"How Will YOU PROVIDE FEEDBACK TO ME WHEN MY HOME SHOWS?"*

I like to contact my sellers with a market update on a regular basis. This may include information about new homes that have come on the market in the neighborhood or changes in pricing that would affect their sale. I also like to discuss with them any showing feedback we've received from buyers or their agents.

In my business, I utilize a third-party tool which sends an email to the showing agent immediately upon their accessing the lockbox. I prefer for my clients to hear the feedback "from the horse's mouth" as I believe it feels more authentic to them. This tool notifies them when feedback is available and allows them to access it online, at their convenience, 24/7.

In the last few years, I have found that many of my client's schedules simply do not allow for weekly face-to-face visits or phone calls. In those cases, the client may prefer information to be shared via text or email. I feel that it is my job to serve the client, so I make every effort to adjust my contact preferences to meet theirs.

> *Hint:* I have heard from many sellers in the past that some listing agents disappear once the listing contract is signed, so this is a very important topic to discuss during the interview as it helps to set an expectation for both you and the listing agent.

## Hold Out for a 20% Agent

We've all heard the old adage "80% of the work is done by 20% of the people". I have found this to be true at church, as well as in any volunteer program I have ever been a part of. It is most certainly true in the real estate industry that 20% of the agents do roughly 80% of the business.

The majority of agents, even those who consider themselves to be full-time agents, often limit the amount of time and effort they are willing to put into building their business. And, that is exactly what it is – a business!

An agent may work for a brokerage, but each agent is an independent entrepreneur. As with any business owner they determine the focus of their business. They determine the amount of time and energy they are willing to put into building their business. They determine the amount of money they will spend marketing their business.

A 20% agent will understand this and have a written business plan in place to ensure success.

A 20% agent will have processes and procedures in place to monitor their business and technology solutions to fully support your listing 24/7.

> **Hint:** Of course your listing agent is going to sleep (and eat and shower), but you do want their marketing to be active around the clock. Don't be afraid to ask how they accomplish this.

# Chapter Two

# How I Sell Homes Quickly & for Top Dollar

Selling your home your home for top dollar comes down to a few very specific issues: marketing, pricing, condition, home availability and property promotion.

**Marketing** is about making your property visible to the buyers most likely to buy it. This is a direct function of the agent and is controlled and managed by them.

**Pricing, Condition and Availability** is about having the property in the best condition possible at the time of listing, pricing it appropriately for the current market and making it easy to show. These are functions managed directly by the seller. You are the only one who can control the price and condition of your home. You are the only one who can make it easy for buyers to see. Of course your agent will gladly provide you with advice and guidance but, at the end of the day, these responsibilities are controlled by you.

**Property Promotion** is about having your property noticed by the agents who are most likely to sell it. This is a function managed by the agent.

# The Importance of Marketing

Property marketing begins long before the house actually hits the MLS. Real estate marketing professionals know that creating a "buzz" about a property before it even comes on to the market is a major step toward getting it closed quickly for the highest price possible.

My marketing strategy launches as soon as the listing is signed and is specifically designed to create momentum in the market place. My "coming soon" promotion lays out specific timelines for myself and the seller and is devised to generate interest in the property immediately. The more interest someone else has in an item, the more the average person wants it. That is just human nature. It is my goal to have homebuyers fighting each other to get in the door on day one, and feeling compelled to make an offer on your home before the next buyer does.

This is accomplished by pushing out high quality marketing collaterals to my own buyer list, as well as by utilizing my network of top-selling local buyer's agents to reach other buyers who are already primed to purchase a home in the area. This may be done personally or through one of my technology driven platforms. It simply depends on the property's location and individual "personality".

**It is my goal to make my listings stand out from the competition.** Every home is unique and a unique property deserves a unique marketing plan designed to best position it in the market. I do that by collaborating with my clients to explore their home's special features and then use my proven marketing techniques to "write a story of the home" which highlights its superior qualities and value. Every home has its own story – the distinctive character, charm and style that made you select it for your home in the first place - that story just needs to be told in a compelling way.

Nothing can do more to bring your home to life, or convey its true appeal, better than a vivid online digital experience and because of that I truly believe that a picture is worth more than a thousand words. As part of my full-service listing program, I include professional, high-definition photography for every listing. The photography staff I use works with me to create a portfolio for the client's home that allows a buyer to fully discover all that the home has to offer. Depending on the location I may also utilize videography, or drone technology, to highlight the unique and special features of a property. As an example, how can you truly present the beauty of a lakefront home without showing a view of the property from the lake? The use of a drone is perfect in this scenario. While the services can be expensive, don't you think you deserve an agent who is willing to invest in your property?

With the Internet playing such a pivotal role in connecting buyers to your home, these are just a few examples of the services you should expect to find in a true real estate marketing professional's marketing plan. You are looking for an agent who offers an unparalleled internet presence and social media exposure. After all, what good are eye-catching photos and glitzy marketing materials if a buyer never actually sees them?

Property marketing is generally paid for by the agent. As you can imagine, this investment creates a strong incentive for the agent to get your home sold.

# Open House or Not?

My answer is almost always YES! This of course depends on your local market. With the strong pre-marketing campaign I employ, my goal is to get the highest number buyers possible in the door, as soon as possible, to create a feeling of urgency.

However, the seller determines property availability. Some are simply not comfortable with a large number of people in their home at one time. Others simply don't like nosy neighbors. My thought on this is "that nosy neighbor may have a friend or family member that wants to live in this neighborhood". Let them see it!! In fact, I generally promote my open houses directly to the neighbors for this reason.

**To help your open house be a success, here are a few seller guidelines to follow:**

- Plan to be out of the house at least 30 minutes prior to the start of the open house to allow the hosting agent time to prepare.

- Remove any extremely valuable items such as jewelry or family heirlooms from the property.

- Remove all firearms and unsecured weapons from the property.

- Remove any prescription medications from the property.

  **Note:** At any given time the agent holding the open house may have several buyers looking at the home. There is simply no way that they can walk through the house with each and every one at the same time. While it is very infrequent that problems occur or items go missing, it is always best to be prepared.

## The Importance of Property Promotion

As I mentioned previously, property promotion is about marketing to other real estate agents -vs- marketing to buyers.

This is an extremely important step in my marketing plan simply because agents are inundated with home listings every day. Most of these listings are very generic and do nothing to make the property stand out from the competition. My goal is to make sure they know that your property is available and are aware of every special feature it offers that might help them target a buyer for it.

Virtually every city has distinct micro-markets which are interesting to different buyer demographics for different reasons. This may be determined by a school district, local amenities, area 'vibe', etc... My goal is to target the agents who sell the most homes in those distinct areas and promote my property listing directly to them.

This information may be provided in person, via email blast or through a direct mail out, but the secret is in knowing who they are and the most effective way to reach them.

# The Importance of Pricing, Condition and Availability

As part of the home selling team, you are responsible for pricing, condition and showing availability.

As I mentioned in chapter one regarding the agent interview, in order to price your home "in the market" a knowledgeable agent will provide you with documented sales (what *real buyers* are paying for homes similar to yours) and market data from multiple sources to help educate you on the current state of market (trending up, trending down or stagnant) and suggest a list price. But, it's what you do with that information that matters.

Many sellers are tempted to price their property above the market value suggested by the listing agent in an attempt to "test the market". Because this higher price screens the property out of the search results for the buyers most likely to purchase it, the seller does not fully benefit from the peak period in which a new listing receives its highest level of interest. Unfortunately, this generally results in the home sitting on the market much longer than it should. A listing which has become stagnant is often seen as a "troubled property" by both buyers and agents which ultimately results in a lower sales price. As you can see, pricing the home properly from day one is imperative to reaching the goal of selling your home in the shortest time possible, for the most money possible with the least amount of stress possible.

In addition to pricing, the condition of the property is solely under the seller's control.

The current deluge of cable channels hosting house flipping and buy/sell renovation shows has proven to be both a blessing and a curse to home sellers. While they can offer homeowners excellent ideas of things they can do to get their home ready to sell, they also set a somewhat false expectation for homebuyers. Homebuyers now walk into homes expecting them to be completely updated with on trend paint colors and flooring choices. While this is somewhat unreasonable, it is a reality that you must consider.

Your agent should provide you with a well thought out list of items that need repair or maintenance attention. I would strongly recommend that you make every effort to comply with any reasonable request. Not doing so could cost you a great deal of money in the end.

But, at the end of the day, no matter how well priced your home is or how hard you've worked to get it into proper selling condition, if it is not available for showings it's not likely to sell.

We all understand that it is inconvenient to leave the house when you have to pack up small children or animals, but in order for a buyer to fall in love with it and buy it, they're going to have to see it. And, the more buyers who see it, the more likely it is to sell quickly.

Many buyers will be coming in the evening after work or on the weekends. Try to be prepared for showings during these times. (It's always the perfect excuse for eating out, because you can't dirty up the beautiful kitchen that is going to sell your house.)

Chapter Three

# Preparing Your House to Sell

Selling your home for top dollar begins with having the property looking its best before the sign goes in and the first buyer arrives. Our goal is to help you get your home sold for the most money possible, in the shortest time possible and with the least hassle possible. To do that successfully, a seller must be willing to see their home through the eyes of a buyer.

## Pre-Sale Preparation

The moment you decide to sell your property the *"home"* you love you must become the *"house"* you are selling. Of course this is easier said than done as most homeowners enjoy a deep emotional connection with their home based on the memories created there.  In order to see your property through the eyes of the buyer you must immediately begin the process of emotionally detaching yourself from it and a change in vocabulary is an easy way to start. We all know that "home is where the heart is", but a *house* is just a product to be sold on the open market.  Keep in mind......**You are getting ready to sell a HOUSE.**

When getting your property ready for market, making the right improvements can greatly enhance your odds of meeting the goal of getting your home sold for the most money possible, in the shortest time possible and with the least hassle possible.  On the other hand doing nothing or making the wrong changes can result in your home sitting on the market longer than necessary and ultimately receiving lower offers.

**Exterior:**  *Curb appeal is your first chance to entice a buyer. Focusing your efforts on the front of the house will greatly enhance its ability to grab a buyers' attention from the start. First impressions are lasting impressions, so you want to be sure that you've done all you can to ensure your house creates a positive first impression.*

Studies show that over 90% of today's buyers use online tools to begin their home search before contacting a buyers' agent. With the vast assortment of listing services and mapping software available, they can easily spend a weekend narrowing down their choices and making a quick drive-by of each.  Your home needs to make a good impression from the moment the buyer sees it from the street if you ever want to have a chance of them seeing the upgraded features it offers inside.

To get started, get into your car and drive around the block. As you drive towards your property, the way a potential buyer would, note your first impressions: Does your house look inviting? Is the landscape neatly trimmed and edged? How about the driveway - are there dirt or oil stains that need to be removed? Can you easily see the architectural features of the house or is it blocked by overgrown trees and bushes? Are there toys and playthings that need to be moved out of sight? Does the mailbox look clean and straight or is it rusty and falling over? Look at the structure - does the home look to be in good condition or does it feel tired and poorly maintained? Make a list of items that need attention.

**These tips will guarantee that your house makes the best first impression possible:**

- Paint your front door. Polish your door and entry hardware. Add fresh plants or flowers and replace the welcome mat. (Buyers will spend several minutes standing here waiting for the agent to open the lock box so it needs to look and feel perfectly maintained).

- Make sure your doorbell is functional.

- Wash or thoroughly clean wood, aluminum and vinyl sided homes. (Pressure washing can remove years of built up dirt, grime and mildew.)

- Rake leaves, trim shrubbery and trees, cut the lawn, and plant a few new, fresh flowers. Put down fresh mulch or pine straw around shrubs and in flower beds.

- Sweep and hose off the walkways and driveways. (Pressure wash, if necessary.)

- Clean the gutters and extend downspouts away from the foundation. (This will come up in an inspection so it's best to take care of it in advance.)

- Organize the garage. Get rid of clutter by either putting it in boxes, or "pre-pack" and rent a storage unit for your garage belongings.

- Check the locks of your home – front entry, back entry, and garage. Sticky locks can give the impression of a home in need of maintenance. And they're often the first thing a buyer sees. A small dab of graphite will make sticky locks work like new.

- Clean oil stains from your driveway and garage with a commercial product.

- Test the garage doors and oil squeaky wheels and tracks.

- Clean up any litter, toys, yard tools or newspapers in the yard or walkways. Remove any leaves in the yard or walkways.

- Touch-up the paint on the exterior of the home if necessary. In some cases it pays to repaint the entire exterior if it hasn't received a fresh coat of paint in years. Hardwood trim on the exterior of the home can make or break its appearance. Make sure it looks clean and appears well maintained.

# Exteriors Attract, But Interiors Sell

Curb appeal draws buyers into your house, but an appealing, well cared for interior will make the sale! While nothing replaces a professional stager when you're getting your home ready for the market, in many cases small tweaks can make a huge difference.

**Interior:** Your house may fulfill all the criteria potential buyers have in terms of location, price, style and amenities but it still needs to make an emotional connection. Inspire buyers by creating scenarios where they can picture themselves. You can do this by creating a "clean slate" using neutral colors in your entryway, living room, family room & dining room. Eliminate excess personal memorabilia and engage all of their senses with soft music and fresh scents. **Just remember - There is no such thing as "too clean" or "too well maintained" when your home is on the market!**

Making minor cosmetic improvements can have a major impact on your final sales price. We often overlook things we see every day which are extremely obvious to a visitor. Make an effort to see your home through the eyes of a buyer. Most buyers want a clean, "move in ready" home and will make MAJOR reductions in their offer price if they feel that repairs or updates are required. Pay attention to deferred maintenance issues that could give the buyer an excuse to reduce the offer price. Find it and repair it before you put your home on the market!

- The entryway sets the first impression so make sure it's in great condition with fresh paint and clean floors.

- Clean out all unnecessary clutter and up to 1/3 of all furniture. (You are selling square footage so let's flaunt what you have!) You want your home to look uncluttered and the rooms to feel open and bright. The average home has too much furniture for showing, and you're going to be moving soon, so you might as well get a head start by "pre-packing" extra furniture, decorative items and any other items you won't be needing before your move.

- Put away knick-knacks and items that make the home look overly personalized. You don't want a buyer feeling that their personality would never fit into the home because they are so overwhelmed by yours. Put away clutter, photos and other objects that will distract buyers. (We want them looking at all that your home has to offer, not your personal items.)

- Sleek and spacious sells - consider renting a storage unit for those extra furnishings, boxes and clutter.

- **Do a thorough interior maintenance review:** Deferred maintenance will cost you money! Oil squeaky doors, tighten doorknobs and latches, replace nonworking fixtures, clean and repair ALL windows, and repair leaking faucets and toilets. Look for chipped paint, cracked drywall or damaged flooring that needs repair.

- Locate ceiling stains and the cause of the leak. (Repair the leak and any visible damage – a major leak will still need to be disclosed, but will cause less concern if repaired).

- It's a good idea to have all windows professionally washed, and clean all window blinds, shades and shutters. (I recommend that you remove and store all window screens to allow in more light and make the house look more welcoming from the street.)

- Replace all burned-out light bulbs and clean lighting fixtures. (Replace cold white or blue light bulbs with styles offering warmer tones.)

- Give your home a spacious look. If you've ever toured a model home, you've noticed that the home is spacious and bright. Make your home look the same by: 1) clearing out stairs and halls of clutter and excess furniture, 2) clear counters in the kitchen and bathrooms, and 3) Make closets and storage areas neat and tidy and like there is room for more. (Buyers will look in the closets and cabinets to see if there is room for their belongings – prove to them there is!)

- Repaint bold colored, non-neutral walls and rooms. (Tinting primer to the new color can make this job much easier).

- Make sure your home is clean by doing the following:

  1) Have carpets professionally cleaned

  2) Clean the refrigerator and stove

  3) Clean and freshen the bathrooms

  4) Clean washer, dryer, and laundry tubs.

(Hire a professional cleaning service, if needed. The money you spend in these areas will come back to you in the form of a higher offer price!)

- Wax or polish wood floors, touch up scratches and glue down any seams, if you have vinyl flooring.

- Make sure windows and doors operate properly and lubricate bi-fold closet door tracks with a silicon spray.

- Glue loose wallpaper seams and remove soiled or damaged wallpaper.

- Clean around fireplaces and remove ashes.

- Organize all closets, pack up unnecessary items for storage, and put all toys away. (Coordinating baskets are a great way to hide "the ugly's".)

- Make sure all beds are made, bedrooms are neat and clean, and all laundry is clean, folded and put away.

- Consider holding a yard sale BEFORE you place your home on the market to get rid of excess items that can make your home look cluttered or small.

- Clean & repair your bathrooms:

1) Repair loose tiles
2) Remove loose grout and apply new grout
3) Remove old tub/tile caulking and replaced with new silicone caulk. Concentrate on areas such as counter corners, shower corners, and the base of the toilet
4) Remove all soap scum and dirt build-up in showers and tubs
5) Clean glass doors and replace badly soiled shower curtains
6) Vacuum exhaust fans. In severe cases, old or damaged tubs can often be sprayed with an epoxy coating.

- Clean & repair your kitchen:

1) Clean ovens thoroughly
2) Clean cooktops, microwaves and exhaust fans
3) Double check all burners to make sure they're working
4) Thoroughly clean the interior of your refrigerator. Remove mold from refrigerator gaskets. Empty the water collection tray under the refrigerator
5) Neatly arrange soaps and cleaning accessories under sink (color-coordinated baskets can prove to be very helpful here)
6) Thoroughly wash cabinets fronts
7) Clean out all cabinets and make sure all handles are securely in place.

## Preparing for your Photoshoot

Photos of your property will be distributed through the MLS and online home search software tools used by buyers. They will likely be the first introduction a buyer has to your home. Buyers will use these photos to create a general opinion of your home and make initial judgements about its maintenance, so it imperative that all possible efforts are made to provide an attractive image.

**BEFORE the photographer arrives:**

**Outside:**

- Mow the lawn and trim back overgrown or dead shrubbery.

- Remove dead potted plants.

- Remove any clutter such as garbage cans, toys, gardening tools, hoses, etc. from sight.

- Make sure the cars are out of the driveway and parked away from the front of the home.

- Clean the areas around any pool, pond or other outdoor feature that will be highlighted.

**Inside: LESS IS MORE...**

- Replace all burned out light bulbs. (The better the lighting, the better the results.)

- Turn on all lights, including lamps, under cabinet lighting, etc.

- Open all blinds/shutters with slats facing up at about a ¾ tilt.

- Clean kitchen counters and remove all counter top appliances such as toasters, microwaves or coffee makers.

- Remove everything from the front or sides of refrigerator (photos, magnets, kid's art, etc.)

- Hide all garbage cans.

- Toilet seats should be down, clean mirrors and other glass surfaces.

- Clear bathroom countertops of all toiletries. Leave only a floral arrangement or house plant.

- Put out the best towels, neatly folded. Do not have any used towels, bathrobes, etc. hanging in the bathroom unless presented neatly on a towel bar.

- Empty the shower of personal hygiene items (shampoos, body washes, razors, scrubbies, etc.)

- Clean & dust everything very well (dust <u>will</u> show in photos)

- De-clutter and dust fireplace mantles.

- De-clutter: try to remove at least half the books, knick-knacks, toys, keepsakes, awards, family photos, kitchen items, off season clothes (makes closets look more spacious), etc. This can extend even to large pieces of furniture in smaller spaces. (Remove pieces that make a room look cramped.)

- Remove any large portrait-sized photographs or paintings, especially over mantles, and replace with more neutral art.

- Minimize extra floor coverings - No small throw rugs as these look like clutter in photos and diminish the perceived room size. Large area rugs are acceptable.

- Remove table coverings, but consider putting out place settings. Remove any towels, pot holders, etc. that may be hanging in the kitchen.

- We all love our pets, but they should be kept out of the way during the photoshoot. Hide feeding bowls, litter boxes, dog beds, etc. Some homebuyers have allergies and can be put-off by the presence of pets.

- Stage the deck/patio - Open patio umbrellas and set out patio furniture cushions (make sure they are clean).

- If in season, uncover grills, pools, spas, and hot tubs (again, be sure they are clean).

- Place dogs in the garage or, better yet, take them to a neighbor's home or doggie daycare for a short visit.

- Make sure that sidewalks, walkways, driveways, etc... are clear of debris and leaves.

- Close garage doors and have no cars in the driveway or directly in front of the house.

- If at all possible, when planning to list your home near any holiday, please decorate with photography in mind. Either schedule the photography session before any decorations go up, or after they come down. No matter what holiday, decorations in the photos will date your listing.

Chapter Four

# Showing Your House to Sell

W hen you know a showing is scheduled, you should put a few last minute touches on your home and spot clean for maximum impact before the buyers arrive. This extra effort can make your home more inviting and appealing, get it sold more quickly and at a better price. The following tips have proven invaluable to my previous sellers and are worth your special attention.

**Showing your home...**

- When leaving the house for the day, leave it as if you know it is going to be shown (many agents don't call until the day of showing – sometimes not until they are in the neighborhood).

- Make the house smell fresh with potpourri, simmering pots or candles. (Go for "clean" smells rather than florals.)

- Make sure <u>all</u> the lights are on.

- Let the sun shine in - open window treatments and blinds. (Dark houses are a major turn off the buyers.)

- Make the beds and remove items from the floors.

- Wipe down the counters, sinks, tubs and faucets.

- Keep the kitchen counters uncluttered and remove dishes from the sink.

- Clean up after your pets. Clean litter boxes frequently and vacuum pet hair. Pet odors have killed many sales!

- Turn off loud, noisy and disturbing television or radio shows. If possible, play soothing background music like an easy listening station. Keep the level low to avoid disturbing the buyers.

- Keep pets out of the way – preferably out of the house. Many people are uncomfortable around animals and may even be allergic to them.

- Leave the premises. Take a short break while your house is being shown. Buyers are intimidated when sellers are present and tend to hurry through the house. Let the buyer be at ease, and allow the agent do their job.

- If you have to stay – step outside – buyers need to feel free to look. **Do not engage the buyers in any way.** The agent knows the buyer's requirements and can better emphasize the special features that may appeal to them. Sometimes a well-meaning seller can thwart a sale with just a few words!

Chapter Five

# When Things Don't Go as Expected

So you've done everything right... You priced your home based on the market comparables, you painted and prepped until your back has given out - so what happened?

## Responding to a Lowball Offer

You just received an offer on your home and you are elated... until you look at it more closely and realize that the offer price is significantly lower than your asking price and the balloon pops. How should you respond?

For most sellers, receiving what they consider to be a lowball offer generates an immediate and, usually, very negative response. For many that response is "This is ridiculous. I'm not even going to respond!" but, any seasoned real estate professional will tell you to **STOP**, before you lose a sale!

Before you choose to ignore any offer on your property you must first stop to think that a written offer means that there is a person who is seriously interested in buying your home and responding with a reasonable counteroffer may well turn that low price offer into a sale with just a bit of strategic negotiation.

In the current market climate I make every effort to prepare my home seller clients for this possibility. In some cases a buyer is just "fishing" to see how motivated the seller is. In others, they simply have the misconception that all areas have suffered the same level of market downturn they have heard the media harp on about.

## *Stop and Think*

No matter how low, all purchase offers deserve a response. In some cases this may be a counteroffer, in others it may be an outright rejection. In order to determine which way is best for your situation, you will need to check your emotions and deal strictly with the facts. A frank discussion with your real estate agent will help you determine the best way to respond and still keep the negotiations open. **Keep in mind: At the end of the day, your goal is to sell your home so you, and your agent, must make every effort to advance the negotiations if possible.** As long as both parties are in discussion there is a chance for a deal to be made. However, once one party declines to respond that chance is gone.

## *Make a Counteroffer*

A counteroffer indicates to the buyer that you are not accepting their offer but you are willing to negotiate. **Curb the instinct to respond at full price.** While real estate "feels" very emotional, in the end, it is a business transaction and the best response is usually a reasoned response.

In most cases, the best strategy is to determine a price and terms that you would readily accept and respond accordingly.

This may mean lowering your price and removing any previously requested seller concessions (such as paying closing costs) or it may mean sticking to your price, but giving in on a few of the buyer's requests (such as leaving behind the new appliances).

## *Review Recent Changes in the Market*

A seasoned agent monitors the local market constantly and should be providing you with market updates periodically throughout your listing period. If they have not already done so, ask your agent to provide you with an up-to-date CMA so you can see which comparable homes in the area have sold since your home was listed or if any new properties have been listed for sale. In an active real estate market, this data is very important as not only the sale price, but the appraisal price may be affected. If the new CMA determines a lower price is warranted based on the recent comps, you might have to lower your price in order to sell.

## *Have Your "People" Call My "People"*

In most cases, the selling agent knows why the buyer made a low offer so request that your agent call them. A buyer's agent cannot necessarily speak to the buyer's "motivation", but if their offer was based on a different set of comps, your agent should be able to get a copy of them for you. If it is simply a situation in which the buyer can't really afford the home he/she wants and is hoping for a desperation sale, then you can feel justified in rejecting the offer and moving on with no more wasted time or effort. Basically, you won't know unless you ask and information is king when negotiating a sale.

In today's real estate climate low offers are more often a "sign of the times" than an actual statement about the quality or value of your home. However, buyers now have access to real estate listings online and most are aware that certain circumstances may make a seller more receptive to a low offer. If your home is vacant or if the wording in your MLS listing signals desperation (motivated seller, seller says bring all offers, etc...) you are much more likely to receive a lowball offer.

If at all possible, try to make your home presentable and reduce any obvious signs that you are overly motivated and the next offer you receive might be more what you have in mind.

Chapter Six

# What Does a Good Listing Agent Do?

**M**any home sellers are not aware of the actual value a Realtor® provides in the course of a real estate transaction. In fact, most consumers have simply never been made aware of the level of expertise, professional skill and plain old hard work that go into successfully completing a real estate transaction.

The list below will provide you with a general idea of the actions necessary for the completion of a successful real estate transaction. The list is not all-encompassing, nor is it an exclusive list of duties as these vary based on the property, but it will provide you with a basic outline of the services you should expect from a full-service real estate agent in return for their professional fee.

**NOTE:** Generally, a full-service brokerage receives no compensation whatsoever until your sale closes.

### Pre-Listing Activities

1. Consult with Seller via telephone regarding their goals, timeframe & circumstances for selling, and set appointment for listing presentation.

2. Research all comparable properties - currently listed properties and recent sales activity - through the Multiple Listing Service (MLS) and/or other public record databases and property valuation sites.

3. Research "Average Days on Market" for comparable properties (both active and closed sales).

4. Create and analyze "trend" reports to determine the current state of the local market and its projected direction.

5. Research and assess the impact of foreclosures in the given neighborhood.

6. Research and assess the impact of any nearby new construction.

7. Download and review property tax information.

8. Obtain copy of property deed(s) to verify property ownership and deed type.

9. Obtain copy of lot survey or subdivision plat/complex lay-out (if available).

10. Obtain copy of HOA guidelines/by-laws (if available).

11. Research property's public record information for lot size and dimensions.

12. Identify Buyer demographic most likely to purchase property

13. Prepare "Comparative Market Analysis" (CMA) based on information collected in previous steps to establish an accurate market value range to assist the Seller in positioning the home to sell.

   a) Identify differences in each property and make price adjustments as needed

   b) Identify all advantages the subject price may have (finished basement, wooded backyard)

   c) Identify any challenges the subject price may have (power lines, steep driveway, etc.)

14. Prepare listing and/or pre-listing presentation package using above materials.

15. Perform a "curb appeal assessment" of the subject property and create a recommendation report.

16. Confirm current public schools and prepare to explain impact of schools on market value.

17. Compile and assemble a formal file on property.

## Listing Appointment Presentation

18. Meet with Seller to provide an overview of current market conditions and trend projections.

19. Review Agent's credentials and accomplishments in the marketplace and explain how this affects their sale.

20. Present Company's profile and position in the real estate industry and how corporate advertising and brand recognition affects their sale.

21. Present CMA results to Seller, including comparables: recently sold properties, pending sales and active listings which are the Seller's current competition on the market.

22. Discuss Sellers assessment of any noted advantage & challenges.

23. Discuss with Seller all property amenities and assess market impact.

24. Provide Seller with a positioning strategy based on the factors of: location, condition, timeframe, marketing and price.

25. Discuss with Seller suggested methods to market the property effectively based on current market conditions.

26. Explain the importance of an effective online marketing strategy based on the current technology driven nature of Buyers in today's marketplace.

27. Explain use of Multiple Listing Service and the importance of the MLS Profile Sheet.

28. Explain the behind the scenes work done by the Agent and the Brokerage staff.

29. Discuss Agent's availability to the Seller, all Buyers' Agents and potential Buyers calling in directly.

30. Explain Agent's role in screening for qualified Buyers to protect Seller from curiosity seekers.

31. Present and discuss strategic master marketing plan in full, once Seller has hired Agent.

32. Review and explain all clauses in Listing Contract and Addendum and obtain Seller's signature.

33. Discuss, and note, Seller's preferred contact method.

## Once Property is Under Listing Agreement

34. Perform a "condition assessment" of the property and suggest changes to help minimize time on market.

35. Identify opportunities where Seller may benefit from neutralizing or depersonalizing specific areas of the home. Make staging recommendation, if necessary.

36. Review results of "curb appeal assessment" with Seller and provide suggestions to improve selling potential.

37. Have Seller complete "Seller's Disclosure" and "Community Association Disclosure" forms.

38. Determine need for lead-based paint disclosure.

39. Complete any outstanding listing contract addendums, exhibits & disclosures and obtain Seller's signature.

40. Prepare detailed list of property's "Inclusions & Conveyances with Sale."

41. Confirm square footage of home via tax records or appraisal.

42. Prepare MLS Profile Sheet – Listing Agent is responsible for quality control and accuracy of listing data.

43. Explain benefits of Home Owner Warranty to seller.

44. Assist Seller with completion and submission of Home Owner Warranty Application, if desired.

45. Confirm that Seller has an active, transferable termite bond on the property.

46. Initiate "Coming Soon" marketing blast.

## Complete "New Listing Checklist" Items:

47. Order Professional photography for use in MLS, property brochures and virtual tour.

48. Load listing data into company transaction management software program to ensure proper tracking.

49. Write an attention grabbing property description for inclusion in MLS, property brochures and other marketing collaterals.

50. Have staff member enter property data from Profile Sheet into MLS Listing Databases (FMLS & GaMLS).

51. Upload property photos into MLS Listing Databases (FMLS & GaMLS).

52. Proofread MLS database listing for accuracy and enter descriptive caption for photos of each room.

53. Load listing data into lockbox software program to allow monitored access to property.

54. Have extra key made for lockbox.

55. Arrange for installation of yard sign(s) and lockbox.

56. Verify if security system is active and note how it operates.

57. Prepare showing instructions for Buyers' Agents and agree on showing times/availability with Seller.

58. Load listing data into (ShowingSuite) Buyer feedback software to provide Seller with feedback.

59. Load photos and listing data into software to create virtual tour.

60. Create and upload property specific webpages for use on Team websites.

61. Design and order full-color property marketing brochures.

62. Create and print "in-home" marketing materials (home book, special feature cards, etc.)

63. Share listing data on social media (Facebook, Twitter, Linked-in, Google+)

64. Create "New Listing" e-blast to email out to top local Buyers' Agents.

65. Update listings on Zillow, Realtor.com, Trulia and the broker's website to "enhance" by adding additional photos, videos supporting documents and custom banners.

66. Write and share new listing blog to generate website SEO.

67. Request that Seller order copy of Homeowner Association bylaws and/or protective covenants, if applicable.

68. Request utility service information from Seller (supplier's name and telephone number).

69. Compile list of all completed repairs, updates and maintenance items.

70. Obtain house plans/floor plan from Seller and copy for property's listing file, if applicable and available.

71. Order plat map for retention in property's listing file.

72. Set up open house date in multiple software programs to push out to internet.

73. Create "Open House" e-blast to send out to top local Buyers' Agents prior to event.

74. When received, place Home Owner Warranty in property file for conveyance at time of sale.

75. Provide Seller with copy of all signed documents and marketing materials.

76. If property is vacant, send "Vacancy Checklist" to Seller.

77. Verify if any portion of the property involves rental units. If so:

78. Make copies of all leases for retention in listing file.

79. Verify all rents and deposits.

80. Inform tenants of listing and discuss how showings will be handled.

81. Refer Sellers to a Realtor® at their new destination, if applicable.

## Ongoing Listing Support

82. Coordinate showings with owners, tenants, and other Realtors®. Return all calls - weekends included.

83. Create open house specific marketing materials and flyers.

84. Hold Open House as soon as reasonably possible.

85. Review comparable MLS listings regularly to ensure property remains competitive in price, terms, conditions and availability.

86. Review trending databases (Trendgraphix, Real Valuator, etc..) regularly to monitor movement within the market.

87. Follow up on feedback from Buyers' Agents as needed.

88. Discuss feedback from Showing Agents with Seller to determine if changes will accelerate the sale.

89. Place regular, scheduled update calls to Seller to discuss marketing and pricing.

90. Reprint/supply brochures promptly, as needed.

91. Promptly enter price and status changes in MLS listing database.

92. Price changes conveyed promptly to all Internet sites.

## Managing the Offer and Contract

93. Receive and review all Offer to Purchase contracts submitted by Buyers or Buyers' Agents.

94. Evaluate offer(s) and prepare to assist the Seller with comparisons.

95. Counsel Seller on offers. Explain benefits and limitations of each offer.

96. Review negotiating strategies with Seller.

97. Contact Buyers' Agents to review Buyer's qualifications and discuss offer.

98. Negotiate all offers on Seller's behalf, setting time limits for due diligence, loan approval and closing date.

99. Prepare and convey any counter offers, acceptance or amendments to Buyer's Agent.

100. When Offer to Purchase Contract is fully accepted and signed by Seller, deliver copies to Buyer's Agent.

101. Confirm Buyer is pre-qualified/pre-approved by speaking with Loan Officer.

102. Obtain pre-qualification letter on Buyer from Loan Officer.

103. Provide copies of contract and all addendums to Closing Attorney.

104. Record and promptly deposit Buyer's earnest money in escrow account if held by the listing agent's broker.

105. Provide copies of Offer to Purchase contract to Lender.

106. Upload copies of signed Offer to Purchase into company transaction management software program to ensure proper tracking.

107. Update MLS and transaction management program to show property is under contract and update showing status.

108. Verify home inspection date and coordinate with Seller.

109. Advise Seller in handling additional offers to purchase submitted between contract and closing.

## Tracking the Loan Process

110. Request copy and verify deposit of earnest money, if not held by the listing agent's broker.

111. Follow-up with Lender on a weekly basis. Assist Buyer with obtaining financing, if applicable.

112. Track loan processing through each step until final underwriter is complete.

113. Relay final approval of Buyer's loan application (clear to close) to Seller.

## **Home Inspection**

114. Ensure Seller's understanding of, and compliance with, Home Inspection Clause requirements.

115. Coordinate Buyer's professional home inspection with Seller and coordinate access to property, if applicable.

116. Verify mold, termite, radon or any other applicable inspections have been ordered if required by contract and coordinate access to property, if applicable.

117. Ensure Seller's compliance with Home Inspection Clause requirements.

118. Review Home Inspector's report and Buyer's request for repairs with Seller.

119. Discuss any required septic system, well flow, etc... report with Seller to assess any possible impact on sale.

120. Deliver any required inspection report to Lender and Buyer's Agent.

121. Enter completion of each task into transaction management tracking software program to ensure proper tracking.

122. Assist Seller with identifying trustworthy contractors to perform any repairs.

123. Verify completion of all required repairs on Seller's behalf, if needed.

## The Appraisal

124. Coordinate appraisal date with Seller and coordinate access to property, if applicable.

125. Provide comparable sales data and information about the property and updates/upgrades to Appraiser.

126. Follow-Up on appraisal.

127. Enter completion into transaction management program to ensure proper tracking.

128. Assist in questioning/rebutting the appraisal report, if the need arises.

## Closing Preparations and Duties

129. Coordinate closing process with Buyer's Agent, Lender and Closing Attorney.

130. Update closing forms and files.

131. Provide Home Owners Warranty confirmation to Closing Attorney's office if required by contract.

132. Ensure all parties have all forms and information needed to close the sale.

133. Confirm closing date, locations and time and notify all parties.

134. Notify Seller of items they must bring to closing (driver's license, etc.)

135. Assist in solving any title problems (boundary disputes, easements, etc.), if applicable.

136. Work with Buyer's Agent in scheduling and conducting Buyer's final walk-through prior to closing.

137. Request final closing figures from Closing Attorney.

138. Confirm that Buyer has received loan commitment "clear to close" at least 3 days prior to scheduled closing.

139. Verify that Buyer's Agent has reviewed closing figures and provided to Buyer for review.

140. Carefully review Seller's closing figures to ensure accuracy of preparation.

141. Review documents with Closing Attorney if errors are found.

142. Provide earnest money deposit check from escrow account to Closing Attorney as needed, if held by my broker.

143. Coordinate this closing with Seller's next purchase and resolve any timing problems.

144. Remind Seller to bring house keys, garage door openers, pool passes etc. to closing

145. Finalize transaction with a "no surprises" closing.

146. Change MLS status to Sold. Enter sale date, price, concessions, Selling Broker and Agent's ID numbers, etc.

147. Close out listing in transaction management program.

## After Closing Duties

148. Coordinate removal of lockbox and signage.

149. Answer any questions and/or resolve any remaining post-closing issues.

150. Respond to all follow-up calls and provide any requested information to clients.

151. Include Seller in all client appreciation events and drawings.

**Let me get this straight,
you sell your watch on Craigslist and
meet the buyer at the police station...**

**But then sell your home by owner
and invite strangers into your house?**

## Chapter Seven

# For Sale by Owner – Is it Worth it?

I completely understand a homeowner's desire to reduce their costs when selling their home. Between making the repairs needed to ready the home for sale and the actual costs involved in buying a new property, a seller can feel overwhelmed as the expenses add up, so putting a little extra money in their pocket sounds like a great idea.

Unfortunately, what many home sellers fail to understand is just how difficult it is to get a qualified buyer in the front door and then successfully complete the rigorous list of tasks required to guide that buyer through the transaction process to final closing.

Additionally, the paperwork involved in a real estate transaction has increased significantly over the years as the requirements for detailed disclosures and lending regulations have expanded. Because of these expanded legal requirements, the rate of sellers choosing to go it alone has dropped appreciatively from a one time high of 19% to a current rate of 8% - the lowest rate on record since the National Association of Realtors® began collecting data.

If you decide to sell your home by owner, there is much to consider so, before you get started, you'll want to ask yourself these questions:

- How will you determine the correct asking price for your home?

- How will you market your home to reach the buyers most likely to purchase a home in your neighborhood? Do you know who those buyers are?

- How will you verify that the buyers who do show up are qualified to buy your home? Do you understand the difference between prequalification and preapproval?

- Is it safe to let strangers into your home?

- How will you access the needed disclosure and contract forms and other sales documents?

- Will you be available during the day to take calls to schedule showings?

- Will you be available during the day to open the house for showings?

- Many buyers are uncomfortable looking at a home when the seller is present. Are you comfortable leaving the home for showings?

- Are you comfortable answering questions about the condition and maintenance of your home? Do you feel comfortable that you can overcome a buyer's objections sufficiently to generate an offer?

- When you receive an offer, how will you negotiate with the buyer?

- Do you feel that you have a full understanding of the real estate purchase contract and its multiple addendums in terms of timelines and contract contingencies regarding inspections and mortgages?

- Will you be available to open the house during the day for multiple inspectors and the appraiser?

- When the inspections are complete how will you negotiate the requested repairs with the buyer?

- How we verify that the buyer's loan is moving forward satisfactorily?

- Do you have a real estate attorney who will assist you in processing the closing?

**This last question is of extreme importance** as even a simple real estate transaction can be laden with potential liability for an unsuspecting home seller. By overlooking even one required form or legally mandated disclosure, a seller can find himself in jeopardy of a long and expensive lawsuit after the transaction closes.

Okay, so you've decided that you feel comfortable marketing your home and completing the needed paperwork. It's a lot of work, but it should certainly pay off for you, right? Maybe not!

What comes as a surprise to many "by owner" home sellers is that the buyers visiting their home know that the seller will be paying a reduced commission and usually expect those savings to be passed on to them through a reduction in the sales price.

**WAIT...** If you're not getting to keep the extra money, why are you putting in the extra effort and taking the legal risks?

Wouldn't it just make more sense to hire a professional... Someone who knows how to market your home and verify the validity of each buyer before they walk in your door... Someone who can keep all of those appointments for you so that you can keep your normal schedule in place... Someone who understands how to negotiate the best possible price for you and keep a transaction moving forward?

In reality, few sellers actually get to keep the money they think they will be saving when selling by owner. Wouldn't it be better to use that money to benefit yourself rather than the buyer?

> **Hint:** Did you know that many real estate agents won't show for sale by owner listings? The extra work involved in completing a transaction with a self-represented seller is significant. Additionally, negotiations can be much more difficult as the seller is emotionally involved with the property and, without the buffer of the listing agent in place, they can become quite intense. In turn, stressful negotiations often lead to failed closings. Failed closings lead to unhappy buyers and few agents are willing to face that possibility.

The National Association of Realtors® offers the following statistics regarding For Sale By Owner sales:

- FSBOs accounted for 8% of home sales last year. The typical FSBO home sold for $210,000 compared to $249,000 for agent-assisted home sales.

**FSBO methods used to market home:**

- Yard sign: 42%

- Friends, relatives, or neighbors: 32%

- Online classified advertisements: 14%

- Open house: 14%

- For-sale-by-owner websites: 15%

- Social networking websites (e.g. Facebook, Twitter, etc.): 15%

- Multiple Listing Service (MLS) website: 10%

- Print newspaper advertisement: 3%

- Direct mail (flyers, postcards, etc.): 3%

- Video: 2%

- None: Did not actively market home: 25%

## Most difficult tasks for FSBO sellers:

- Understanding and performing paperwork: 12%

- Getting the right price: 6%

- Preparing/fixing up home for sale: 6%

- Selling within the planned length of time: 18%

- Having enough time to devote to all aspects of the sale: 6%

**Source: 2015 National Association of REALTORS® Profile of Home Buyers and Sellers

Chapter Eight

# Expired Listings – What Happens Now?

*My Listing Has Expired and So Has My Patience...*

Having a home on the market for a prolonged period without a closed sale can be extremely frustrating. In a weak real estate market the delay is easy to understand, but when sales in the local market are strong and your home just sits there it can feel personal.

It's important to keep in mind that no home is unsellable. It just requires finding the right combination of price, condition and marketing.

The first step in determining why your home didn't sell is to ask yourself a few questions:

**Was it the house?**   Your previous listing agent should have made you aware of any issues, or obvious shortcomings, they believed would adversely affect the sale of your property. Additionally, they should have provided you with a list of any repairs or updates that needed to be completed prior to your home going on the market.

- Did you make the changes requested or are there still significant updates needed?

- Have you made all needed repairs?

- Is the house clean and decluttered?

- Does the house smell fresh or are there lingering tobacco or pet odors?

- Are there any obvious shortcomings that you are aware of in terms of location (noisy roads, power lines, etc.)?

- Did you receive negative feedback from potential buyers that you have not acted upon?

If the house and lawn are picture-perfect and there are no negative attributes to the location then we must keep looking.

**Was it the agent?** Your previous listing agent should have provided you with a marketing plan prior to your agreement being signed. This plan should've clearly defined the steps they would take to promote your property to local showing agents and potential buyers.

- Did the agent use a professional photographer/ videographer?

- Did the agent provide a virtual tour of your property?

- Did the agent's signage look professional?

- Did the agent provide professionally designed and printed marketing materials?

- Did the agent use visual words and expressive descriptions to bring your home to life?

- Did the agent aggressively use Internet technology to promote your listing?

- Did the agent use technology (such as an e-blast) to promote your listing to top producing buyers agents in the area?

Gone are the days when putting in a sign and listing a property in the MLS was sufficient. With over 90% of home buyers starting their search on the Internet, it is extremely important that your listing agent be well-versed in technology and capable of explaining to you how they use it as part of their marketing program.

Agents who are not aggressively marketing their listings are members of what I call RELAX Realty - they put a sign in your yard and they RELAX!

In this day and age, there is simply no room for a lazy agent. There are too many agents willing to work hard and earn your business. If your previous listing agent was a member of the RELAX Realty crowd, I suggest you find a new one!

So, if the house looks great and your agent aggressively marketed the property then we have to go one step further, and it can be a tough one for many sellers to accept.

**Was it you?**   In some cases a seller can actually make what should be an easy to sell home virtually unsellable. Your listing agent should have provided you with detailed showing instructions to help you prepare your home to look its best when buyers arrive.

- Did you follow those suggestions? Was the house in show ready condition when the buyers arrived?

- Did the curb appeal welcome them from the street?

- Did you turn on all of the lights and have the house smelling fresh?

- Was the house clean?

  o Were the beds made?

  o All clothes picked up?

  o Kitchens, bathrooms and floors gleaming?

- Were there animals in the home?

- Did you limit availability or make it difficult for buyers to see your home?

- Did you have other requirements that made it difficult for an agent to show your home?

- Did you leave the property for showings so buyers felt comfortable looking?

Sometimes even well-meaning sellers can harm their efforts to sell. I always recommend that my sellers leave the property so the buyers feel comfortable and aren't made to feel as if they are snooping. It is also not uncommon for a seller to bring up something that turns the buyer off. Something you see as a positive for your property may actually be seen as a negative by a buyer. It is best that you are away from the property and allow the sales professional working with them to do their job.

**Was it the price?** As I've mentioned in prior chapters, price is king when it comes to selling real estate. Because of this, I feel that it is imperative that a new CMA be completed on your home before it is reintroduced to the market.

If the property is in good condition, it was properly marketed based on the examples I've provided and you have made it easy to show, then you must strongly consider that the price is simply out of line with what a real buyer is willing to pay for a similar home in your market.

An honest assessment of the topics listed here in chapter 8 should help you find clarity in regard to how you can move forward and get your home sold!

# Chapter Nine

# The Buying Process

T he process of buying a home can be summarized in the following steps.

1. Choosing Your Realtor®

2. Coordinating Your Financing

3. Starting Your Home Search

4. Preparing Your Purchase Offer

5. Arranging the Inspections

6. Completing the Financing Process

7. Settlement Details

8. Completing the Final Walk Through

9. The Closing

## #1 Choosing Your Realtor®

As Georgia real estate laws have changed and expanded over the last few years, the true value of using a "buyer's agent" has become increasingly more evident. While there are no disadvantages to a utilizing a buyer's representative, the benefits can be considerable, and I consistently see more home buyers electing to have a Realtor® represent their interests during the home buying process.

In almost all cases, the commission paid to the buyer's agent is paid by the seller. This amount is determined in advance (at the time the property is listed) and is paid to the listing agent's broker or real estate company. A portion that fee is then dispersed to the buyer agent's real estate company at closing.

As the commission amount is pre-determined, it is easy to see why taking the buyer's agent out of the equation will generally save money for neither the buyer nor the seller. However, doing so leaves the buyer completely unrepresented while making one of the most important investment decisions of their life.

## Your Realtor® Should:

- Have a thorough understanding of the real estate industry

- Have extensive education and a proven track record backed by real life experience in the real estate business

- Be knowledgeable of the local market as well as the specific neighborhood in which you are looking for a home

- Be a good communicator and communicate in the manner that you prefer - for example email, texting or phone calls

- Have exceptional negotiating skills

- Be able to deal with challenges as they arise in a calm and mature manner

- Have exceptional interpersonal skills, allowing them to work well with you as well as any cooperating agents involved in the transaction

- Be accessible and available to you for any and all questions or concerns

- Have a good reputation in the industry and be able to provide you with references from previous clients

According to the National Association of Realtors®, when a buyer uses a Realtor®, when buying their home they generally find the home an average of one month faster and have access to far more homes than those who do not use a Realtor®.

## Options for Agent Representation

*'caveat emptor' – let the BUYER BEWARE*

Georgia law requires that the relationship between the buyer and the real estate agent assisting them is spelled out clearly. Here is a brief description of each type of agency allowed:

### No Agent Representation:

Yes, you can actually choose to have no representation at all. Many buyers believe that they will get a "better deal" by working directly with the listing agent of a property. However, that is generally not the case. The commission amount is pre-determined by the listing agreement which spells out what the seller will pay in commission whether there is one agent involved or two.

In this case, the listing agent has a written agreement with the seller and, while the law states that they must deal fairly with all parties, they represent only the seller's interests. As a buyer, it only makes sense that you need your own professional representation and counsel.

> **Hint**: Think of it this way, you'd never hire your spouse's attorney to represent you in a divorce. The listing agent is the seller's representative. You deserve to have someone looking out for you!

## Agent Representing Buyer as a Customer:

In this case, the buyer will work with an agent other than the listing agent, but does not want to use this agent as their exclusive buyer's agent. This greatly limits what the agent can do in terms of providing information, helping you to determine a price and negotiating. In this case, the agent can simply open the homes and complete the contract paperwork based on information  provided by the buyer. The agent cannot assist the buyer in determining the offer price. In this type of representation, a buyer will be asked to sign a GA real estate form called the Agreement to Work with Buyer as a Customer.

## Agent Representing Buyer as a Client:

In this case, the buyer will have a written Buyer Brokerage Agreement with an agent who agrees to fully represent the buyer's best interest at all times in regard to:

- Protection of the Buyer's private information

- Coordination of the lenders and other service providers as needed

- Research and assistance in structuring an offer (reasonable price, terms and conditions)

- Negotiating favorable contract terms for the buyer

- Share all material facts they may be aware of regarding the seller's circumstances and the property's condition.

**Hint** - Using the trusted professionals recommended by your agent (lenders, closing attorney's, etc...) offers you the greatest possibility of completing your transaction in a timely fashion with less risk of errors or surprises. A seasoned agent would only recommend a service provider with a proven track record for success. In addition, service providers who have a history of working with your agent understand that future business is on the line which gives your agent more leverage should a problem arise. On the other hand, a "one off" service provider, who knows that it is unlikely they will receive future business from the agent, feels less pressure to perform.

## Designated Agency:

Designated Agency occurs when a Buyer's agent sells an in-brokerage listing. This is not an unusual situation. In this case, one agent will solely represent the seller and the Buyer's agent will solely represent the buyer. The agents must keep the transaction at "arms length" and may not share

71

information between the parties without prior written permission.

**Dual Agency:**

Dual Agency occurs when a listing agent sells their own listing and attempts to represent BOTH the buyer and seller. As I feel that it is impossible for me to impartially represent the best interest of two separate parties at the same time, I do not practice dual agency.

# #2 Coordinating Your Financing

Prearranging your financing is very important in determining what your home buying budget will be. As you begin speaking with various lenders they should provide you with a "loan estimate" form which spells out the actual costs of the various fees involved in them providing the loan for you as well as their stated interest rate for your loan type. These fees can vary significantly from lender to lender so you will want to pay strict attention to them.

A lender should be willing to take time to discuss with you your current financial situation, the funds you have available for closing and which loan type best suits your needs.

If you have any questions about financing, your agent should be able to refer you to trusted lenders that she has worked with before.

> **Hint** - Choose your lender based on their reputation, availability and trustworthiness and not just the interest rate!

Once you have selected the lender you will be working with, you will want to begin the loan application process as soon as possible so the lender can provide you with a pre-approval letter. Having a preapproval letter helps your agent negotiate with the seller for the very best price and terms as it shows the seller that you are a serious buyer who is well qualified to close. Buyers who choose to write a contract without being preapproved for financing generally find themselves at a competitive disadvantage.

**Preapproval is different than prequalification.** When you have preapproval from your lender, that means that you have actually applied for the loan, provided the required documentation for vetting and have been approved by the lender. Prequalification, on the other hand, means that you qualify for a loan based on the undocumented information you have provided, but you have not yet submitted your documents or been approved and the lender has not made any guarantees to you.

Your lender will provide you with a more definitive list, but here are some of the items you should be prepared to provide:

- Proof of employment (W2's for the last 2 years)

- Proof of previous employment

- Copies of bank, savings and investment account statements

- Information regarding additional income sources which may include things like Social Security benefits, rental income, child support, etc.

- Permission to request your credit report

- Auto loans

- Credit card debt

- Other assets and liabilities

- Tax returns

The pre-approval letter will generally be contingent on a few things: usually a full appraisal, inspections, and title search.

## Money Matters: Other things you need to know

- The higher your credit score, the lower your interest rate will be on your loan.

- You will need to be prepared to pay closing costs which are approximately 3% of the price of the home. In some cases it can be negotiated for the seller to pay all or a portion of your closing costs, but you need to be prepared to pay the full amount yourself.

- The "mortgage payment" provided by the lender may not include taxes and insurance. You will want to make sure you verify those amounts.

- Every home has property taxes associated with it. At the very least you will pay a county property tax, and in some cases you may be required to pay a city property tax as well.

- If you are buying a condominium or a house with a homeowners association you will also have monthly/yearly association fees.

- Depending on your financial circumstances you may receive tax benefits as a result of buying a home. Check with your accountant or tax advisor.

## Homeowners Insurance

As you most likely already know, all homes that are not fully paid off require homeowner's insurance (though it only makes sense for <u>every</u> homeowner to cover their potential risk of loss through the purchase of homeowners insurance). Collectively, "homeowner's insurance" provides hazard insurance, liability coverage and contents coverage for the owner. You will need to contact your current insurance company or insurance broker to set up the insurance policy. **Do not wait until the last minute** as the insurance underwriting process can take longer than many buyers realize. In order to determine their potential risk the insurance company must consider your past claims history as well as any unique issues related to the new home; for example, it's location, if it has a specific type of roof, etc. and this determination takes time. You do not want to delay your closing, or pay a higher rate, by not acting on this in a timely fashion.

## #3 Starting Your Home Search

The most important aspect of your home search will depend on your ability to clearly state your needs and wants to your agent.

Your agent's goal is to find the houses that most closely fit your needs in order to limit the time needed to complete your search and get you settled into your new home with as little stress as possible.

I remind all of my clients that the homes we will be seeing are not my home. I did not decorate them and the more honest they can be with me about what they like or don't like about a house makes it much more likely that I will be able to find them the perfect home in a timely fashion.

So, be completely honest with your agent about what you need and what you want. It will save you a lot of time in the long run and certainly reduce the stress level of all parties.

# Finding your ideal home

The next thing you need to do is be completely honest with yourself. During your search, you may find that some of the things that you thought you couldn't live without might turn into things you can actually do without. Sometimes your 'wants' simply go beyond your budget. Your 'wants' can be a good starting point, but expect your wish list to change during the time that you are looking for houses with your agent.

You will also want to determine where you need to be. This may be limited by choice of a specific school district or your proximity to work. If commute is an issue, I suggest that you determine the maximum distance you are willing to drive and limit your search to those communities.

# #4 Preparing Your Purchase Offer

Once you have found a home that you love, the first thing your agent should do is prepare a comparative market analysis (CMA) to determine a reasonable value for the home.

At this time you should make your agent aware of any special needs you may have regarding the terms and conditions of the contract (such as closing date, amount of the earnest money, extra time needed to complete inspections due to travel requirements, etc.)

You will then strategize with your agent to structure an offer which maximizes your potential of receiving a positive response. Once this is agreed, the agent will prepare the offer for your signatures and present it to the listing agent. A specific time period will be allotted for their response.

The contract will include many important timelines (such as due diligence, inspection and lending time frames) that must be met or extended in writing with the agreement of all parties. It's very important that your agent discusses each of these with you and explains the possible consequences should you not meet these dates. Some can void your contract and some can cost you money!

> **HINT:** In the past, I recommended that my buyers write a personal letter to the home seller that told the story of who they are and why they want to buy the house. In fact, we often included a family picture. Unfortunately, due to changes in the fair housing laws, this is no longer an acceptable practice. If a buyer chooses to do so outside the transaction they can, but the agent cannot be a party to it.

**This is when the negotiating begins!** After your offer is presented to the seller it will either be accepted, rejected, ignored or the seller will submit a counter offer. If they make a counter offer that means that they are willing to negotiate, but they have made some changes to the offer. A specific time period will be allotted for you to respond. You will speak with your agent regarding the best option for you and either accept the seller's counter offer or respond back with a counter offer of your own. Long, protracted negotiations are generally not the first choice of anyone involved, but there are times where they are needed.

Once the buyer and seller reach an agreement, your agent should coordinate with your lender to confirm everything is in order for them to proceed with your financing and you will then schedule any inspections you feel are necessary. If you do not have a list of trusted service providers your comfortable working with, your agent should be able to provide referrals for local vendors and then be available to coordinate access and address any concerns you may have.

> **HINT:** I always work to make my client's offer as attractive as possible to the home owner in case multiple offers are in play on the home. This is not an unusual situation in our area and it is my goal to make sure that our offer stands out and is ultimately chosen. I always strive to write a very clear offer with few stipulations so that it is easy for everyone involved to understand and creates no undue concern for the seller. Of course, as we discussed earlier, you can make your offer even more attractive by including a copy of your commitment letter from your lender. Depending on the current market and location of the house, you may be able to negotiate a price that is lower than asking price and sometimes you may be forced to offer more than the listing price in order to get the home. In both cases, a clear, concise and respectful offer can prove to be worth its weight in gold.

## My negotiating philosophy

There are many factors that go into negotiating on a home, but I always look at what is most important to my clients. It could be a favorable closing date; it could be a playset in the backyard that the kids fall in love with or it could be all about price... it really depends on the clients. At the end of the day, I am a tough negotiator and it is my goal to negotiate in such a way that my clients get what they want. That being said, the best deals are formed when all parties feel that the negotiations are done in a fair, reasonable and respectful way.

Occasionally I will have a client who wants to submit an extremely low offer, just to "test the waters". There can be multiple reasons for this, but in most cases they simply want to make sure that they're not paying more than they absolutely have to for the home. Unfortunately, sellers can be very emotional about the sale of a much loved home and an extremely low offer can be seen as personally offensive.

I warn all of my buyers that by putting in an offer that is so low as to create a negative emotional response in the seller, they will never get the lowest price they could have otherwise. I have seen sellers refuse to sell their home to someone who later came back with a generous offer just out of spite. I believe that it is in the buyer's best interest to structure a fair and respectful offer that allows all parties to work together toward a successful transaction. Keep in mind, you will be negotiating with them again during the inspection phase.

# #5 Arranging the Inspections

There are a wide variety of home inspections that can be conducted. A general home inspection is highly recommended and, depending on the size of the home, usually takes 2 to 4 hours to be completed. The home inspection - conducted by a licensed home inspector - can bring to light any major problems with the home that may cause you to amend your offer or even walk away from the purchase entirely.

In areas known to have high radon gas levels, a radon inspection is generally conducted. In addition, you may choose to have other property specific systems such as well or septic tanks inspected.

Upon completion of all inspections you will receive a full report for each. Depending on the outcome, you may wish to request that the home seller repair certain items of concern as a condition of the contract. These are items to be negotiated.

## #6 Completing the Financing Process

Your lender will need to receive a fully signed copy of the sales contract, including all listed exhibits. If you do not have this, your agent should provide it to you.

Your lender will also need the previously discussed documents required for the loan. If you are already preapproved then you have likely already provided them, but you will want to confirm this.

The lender will order an appraisal of the home to confirm an accurate market value as it relates to the contract.

Per federal financing laws, your lender must provide you with a full loan disclosure at least three business days prior to the closing. It is very likely that they will have you log into an encrypted server to accept the documents and provide e-signatures. Not having this completed within the time frame allotted will result in a three day delay so please sign them immediately upon request.

# #7 Settlement Details

It is generally the buyer who selects the closing attorney to conduct the settlement of the home sale, but it must be one that is approved by the lender. The date of the closing should be arranged as soon as possible as closing offices are usually very busy on Fridays and during the last week of every month. This is usually coordinated by your agent.

## What you need to provide for closing

- A bank wire in the amount of the down payment and your closing costs should arrive in the closing attorney's account 24 hours prior to the closing time. The closing attorney will provide wiring instructions to you via an encrypted email source.

- Proof of payment for a 12 month home owner's insurance policy, if it has not been provided by your carrier.

- Most closing offices will require two forms of ID. One must be your driver's license or passport. The other may be something more simple such as a library card or big-box store membership card.

- Any other items specifically requested by the closing attorney.

Your agent should attend the closing with you so check with them in advance if you have any questions.

Gayle Barton

## Title insurance

I recommend that all of my clients purchase title insurance. The lender will require that you purchase a policy for them and it only makes sense that you protect yourself as well.

The term 'title' is a statement of property ownership. When you buy a home the title is transferred to you as the new owner. On any property a "title defect" could arise which is anything in the history of that real estate property which may encumber your rights to the title without you even realizing it.

Title insurance protects you against unforeseen risks which may not come up in the original title search. Speak with the closing attorney early on regarding their policy. **In some cases a survey is required in order for the title insurance to provide full coverage.** Surveys often take up to three weeks and you do not want to delay your closing by not having it completed in a timely fashion if it is needed.

# #8 Completing the Final Walk-Through

Your contract will allow for you to conduct a final walk through of the home prior to closing. This is usually done 24 to 48 hours prior to the closing. The inspection is usually performed after the seller has vacated the property but prior to you taking possession of the property. You want to verify that all the items that were included in your offer are present in the home. You also want to make sure that the property is in roughly the same condition as when you saw it and originally placed your offer.

# #9 The Closing

The law now requires that the buyer must receive the final closing disclosure from their lender at least 3 days prior to the closing date. This document will display all of your costs associated with obtaining the loan and buying the home. It will also tell you the amount of money you'll need to wire to the closing attorney's office prior to the date of closing.

Hopefully, the attorney's office will have the information needed to provide your agent a copy of the final settlement statement as well so both you and your agent have time to examine it and discuss any questions you may have. However, it is not unusual to see it for the first time on the day of closing.

You will need to make sure that any issues that arose during the walk-through have been taken care of before you attend the closing. Please be aware that settlements are usually scheduled every hour of the day so it's important to allow for an hour to complete the settlement. Try to avoid a settlement late in the day because it might not settle until very late or possibly even the next day.

The most important thing to note in the buying process is that your Realtor® should be with you every step of the way. They are there to guide you, counsel you, and protect you. Trust that their years of experience will help you have the most favorable outcome when buying a home.

# Conclusion

Whether buying or selling a home you need an experienced, professional representing your best interests!

Don't be afraid to ask questions or set expectations. An experienced agent will be more than prepared to discuss any concerns you may have and answer any questions about themselves or their business.

I hope the information I have provided empowers you to take control of your future real estate transactions and benefit fully from the professionals who you hire to assist you.

*Gayle Barton*

Additional information can be found on my website at www.BartonTeamRealEstate.com.

# What People Are Saying About Gayle Barton

I cannot recommend Gayle highly enough. She is by far the best real estate agent I have ever dealt with. She is honest, hardworking and relentless in helping you find what you are looking for. She is truly the only agent I have ever used that I felt was 100% working on my behalf. If you are ever in need of an agent to help you buy or sell a home, look no further.
- *Craig B.*

Gayle did a fantastic job selling our home. She explained the demographics, area competition as well as the process of how we would sell our home. Her pictures were fantastic and the video virtual tour was hands down the best that we have ever seen. Her premarketing plan was so good that we had appointments waiting to see the home the day it listed. We got an over list and a full price offer on day one and a total of 7 offers in 4 days, including two over list. Gayle knew how to price us "in the market" so that it drove those full and over list offers from day one. We cannot recommend Gayle with any more fervor, she was awesome and will be for you as well.
- *Jason W.*

Gayle was wonderful to work with! She is very knowledgeable and professional, and it is very obvious she cares about finding her clients a home they'll be happy in, and not just in making a sale. She helped us navigate the process of both buying and selling a home, and alleviated any burdens that she could! She has an excellent marketing approach, and I believe that

her strategies in both showing our home and tips for us in preparing our home for sale were what got us an offer so quickly. We had already found our next home, so we were thrilled to receive MULTIPLE offers within days of our open house, many over our asking price. I would highly recommend Gayle to anyone looking to buy or sell a home.
- *Morgan J.*

We absolutely loved working with Gayle! She is very responsive and was always looking out for our best interests. Everyone needs Gayle in their corner!
- *John L.*

Working with Gayle was a joy. She sold our home and helped us find the perfect new home. During that time she kept us informed and up to date. If we had questions she would answer them or find the answer for us. She takes an interest in her clients and makes them feel like they are number one in importance. Her calming spirit is a delight.
- *Marsha K.*

We liked Gayle's work so much the first time we purchased a home with her that we came back for more three years later. She is very knowledgeable, efficient and honest in her dealings. Her high energy and tireless work ethic make her a joy to work with. She treats her clients with respect and listens to her clients concerns and preferences. We would highly recommend Gayle to anyone.
- *Keith G.*

Gayle was awesome to deal with. We went through 3-4 agents before finally landing on an agent that was willing to work with us and give an incredible effort (we even had one agent tell us our price point wasn't worth her time). We were under time constraints, ran into issues with the home we were purchasing, etc. and she was always a pleasure to work with. I would highly recommend Gayle to anyone looking for a reliable and hardworking agent.

*- Chris K.*

My wife and I were relocating due to a new job. Finding a home in a brand new state/city can be very challenging. We also had a tight timeline. We worked with Gayle remotely ahead of time selecting potential area/houses and with her knowledge of the market/area she was able to help us to narrow/define the area. She dedicated multiple days with us and prescheduled all the showings for consecutive days. Within one week's time in GA we are able to select an awesome house that we now love. She was a big help in every step of the process. We highly recommend Gayle!

*- Bryan S.*

I'm very happy to give Gayle my highest recommendation. She is extremely knowledgeable, diligent, responsive and very patient with her clients. I found working with her a joy and felt she was there to help during every step of the process. Gayle is a true professional and she loves her job!!

*- Cassie M.*

Gayle was so responsive and knowledgeable about our sale! She made it very easy on us and removed the stress from our real estate transaction. Thank you Gayle!

*- Kristen M.*

Gayle deserves the highest recommendations. We greatly enjoyed the entire shopping and purchase process with her as our Realtor. She was able to provide custom lists of homes for us to review prior to our visit. The active market and our tastes allowed us to quickly narrow down the homes we were interested in. She arranged several showings of both existing

homes and new constructions and her vast experience was obvious when we discussed purchase options. Even after our closing she has continued to be super responsive to questions and has helped with every request. We are most pleased and again can highly recommend her.
*-Brian M.*

Working with Gayle has been a wonderful experience. She has been helpful through the entire process of selling our house. She was always available and quick to respond. She helps walk you through the process of offers/counter offers and gives sound advice. I highly recommend her as an agent and know I would use her again if needed. Our house sold in two weeks!
*-Ann W.*

After just closing on my new (first) home, I can say without a doubt that I will not even consider another Realtor if I end up moving in the future. I had already referred Gayle to several coworkers before I even closed on the home.

She met and exceeded my expectations every step of the way. Making every possible attempt to meet all of my demands, both the home search and following in person meetings were a breeze. Every bit of communication was prompt, usually faster than even my significant other's.

As the buyer, Gayle was able to negotiate far better terms than I had even considered possible.
*- Cody B.*

We were moving to a new area that we did not know and Gayle did a great job in giving us a total perspective of the area. She knows Forsyth County! She was always well prepared and was very aware and receptive of our needs and found the house that we were looking for. She is very strong on follow-up and

responds quickly. She was always available to us for house hunting. She works in a very positive and professional manner. She just did a great job, we highly recommend her.
- Ed S.

I contacted Gayle at the last minute to help us with an offer on a new home. Not only was Gayle extremely responsive, she got us in touch with a lender who was able to secure financing in a very short amount of time. Throughout the entire process, she was fantastic to work with. Based on that process, we decided to use her to list our existing home. Within the first week, over 20 families saw our home and we had an offer within the first 10 days. Gayle was patient, walked us through the entire process, and provided guidance at the appropriate time. We are going to use her again to list our parent's house and are looking forward to working with her. I would strongly recommend Gayle to anyone either looking to buy or sell a home.
-Ryan G.

Working with Gayle was great. She knows what it takes to sell houses and "get it done". We basically set the price and she was off and running, getting our home visible in the marketplace. When we received an offer, again, it was so simple as she knows what steps to take, and doesn't waste any time.

Gayle knows the market, the process and all the players in the real estate market.
- Liz B.

My husband and I have bought and sold homes a number of times during our 33 years of marriage. Never have we had a better, more knowledgeable or more responsive agent than Gayle Barton. We have and will continue to recommend Gayle

to friends and family for all of their real estate needs. We could not have been more pleased with every aspect of her work on our behalf. SHE IS ONE IN A MILLION!!
- *Jane L.*

Since we're out of town most of the time, we left our home in Gayle's capable hands. We never felt out of touch because the viewing results of our property were communicated immediately to us through a feedback link on her website. We highly recommend Gayle and her staff to anyone who wants a professional proactive Realtor that will produce results quickly.
- *Sherry E.*

Read more customer reviews on Zillow or at her website at www.BartonTeamRealEstate.com

45780982R00054

Made in the USA
San Bernardino, CA
17 February 2017